REVISED EDITION

It's Mother's Day

POEMS 1990-1995

ROGER APLON

Marc Chagall In Venice

The layering of fish
inside the trattoria's glass & stainless case,
makes Chagall's sketch of a trout
throbbing in the young man's pants
as he dreams of some lost love
very much a meal.

A quick bite to delete the twinge of lust fermenting
in this Venice damp.
Each rolled Sole,
each Flounder,
every Hake

glaring
from chipped ice,
squeezed by lemons, kale & gouts of parsley
wets the appetite for the distilled,
100 proof juice of sex.

Venice in May: All the reds & blues & yellows
of his palette, exploding in a rainbow
smack at the center of St. Marc
Square & Marc Chagall
not one to avoid

desire, never to deny the fish a place at table,
if not bed, is at home here, baiting
our hooks & hanging out

like his Russian
drawings,

Full of steamy jokes & cravings of the flesh.

The Virgin In The Tree

After a print by ***Paul Klee***

They found her in a tree.
She'd wriggled out on a branch.
By the second day thirst got her
followed by hunger
& barking dogs.

In June, on the night of the new moon
she drank at our trough, bit a hunk
from the ear of our young sow.
No one has ever seen her clothed
her skin, at a distance, leathery & stained . . .

It took two of us to bring her down.
Old folks & kids tossed tomatoes. She only chuckled,
gave an upraised finger to all who dared pass by.
With the onset of winter, she'd burrowed under
sacks of barley, ignored offers of affection.

Sightings began again that fall.
Adolescent girls were the first to notice:
flicker of thigh, a taunting breast, hint
of her scent on thinning air.
No one's ever tried to explain

her eventual disappearance.
One cloudy night, assumed dry lightening
lit a patch of brush to flickering then fade.
Soon, the town went back to normal. Was
never the same again.

She Makes My Day

In Memory of ***Ai***
Mistress of Words-as-Weapons

That's a mighty posture you wear, Lady.
Framing a defiance only
the brave or those

confident enough to run from home
could wear well. Like a diver
poised in midair

arches her body just enough / to tip the scales
you turn the obvious to dark
surprise. I relish your

J. Edgar & your Clarence T. rubbed
thin-skinned to the bone,
naked as jelly.

Just as fractured as you've left them
hot to the touch, cold on
the plate. I delight

in your refusal to fly while sailing
all over the map of my
all too searing

rage. Leaping into our tidy graves like a master
shit disturber you scrub away
platitudes,

peel back our clouded corneas, air out
the tent, like a good emetic
relieves congestion.

Jim Talks About Coyote Mask

For Jim Allen who owned the relic & knew its powers

I can't believe she'd want to give it up.

Bad vibes, she said. Too dark.
Or some such nonsense. I think power.

The dancer with the cunning tongue
mesmerizing rattlers, toads & puma alike.

I picture him totally out of control

rabid: head wagging
frothing at the mouth

goatee flecked with spit
smacking his lips & licking his gums

terror waiting out of reach
to snatch away your kill.

No wonder Zuni treasure tales of his treachery

why he's mascot to despair. Bobbing & weaving, he circles & all eyes follow.

He's been known to tease, to change his shape, disappear / appear again.

There are those who've seen him dining at the finest tables /

blessed by the most elaborate churches.

My neighbor recounts that time in the desert: She'd waited to be rescued from the cold

Coyote took her to his den, fed her a hot meal then mounted her

letting loose a tantalizing truth she'd been forced to deny for years.

"Power" Did I say.

He holds the lever / turns it at his pleasure

singing yip-yip-yip-a-we
YIP-YIP-YIP CO - YO - TE!

Family Bonds

Growing up human is uniquely a matter of social relations rather than biology. What we learn from connections within the family takes the place of instincts that program the behavior of animals; which raises the question, how good are these connections?

Elizabeth Janeway: 1981

Father & Son

Bill Browne's dad would whip out the old cat-o-nines & after a dozen pints & railing against the Jews, beat the shit outta Bill. What a guy. & Bill, learning to hate all kike kids, would bash his hands through doors & walls cursing & shredding his bloody knuckles, while his rumpled old dad stumbled down Cornell Avenue or Ridgeland Avenue or Harper Avenue, shamrock pinned to his lapel & trusted shillelagh rapping the sidewalk stride for stride / six-sheets-to-the-wind, pissing his pants & shouting "fuck the niggers" at anyone he'd come upon. Bill had fixed on chasing us smaller than him, wielding flat-end baseball bats or bike chains or a broke-necked bottle & . . . But / It was then / When Bill got hung-upside-down out their third floor window & dropped, his mom drove a kitchen knife into the old man's back. Once paroled, she caught the first flight to Ireland & a bitter but redeeming peace . . . Occasionally – we'd still see the old man sleeping-one-off in Jackson Park or on 67th Steet beach.

& then

After-a-while

not at all

O Yeah!

It wasn't so unusual Pops drinking most of the afternoon & when Ma would send me

I'd go to the bar & take him out the back. It was always nip & tuck getting home.

When he'd wake he'd try to thank me / barf all over my clean dress..

Out of work for years & broke, he'd booze on credit, do odd jobs for the bill. Sometimes he'd take me along, the cab of the truck smelling of piss & gasoline.

I'd hang out the window for a whiff of fresh air.

After I turned 13 he taught me how to hold a cue & how to make a perfect bridge with my small hand spread wide,

how to grip the butt-sleeve, with just the tips of me fingers, make long, slow, decisive strokes / how to hit the balls dead on.

We'd drive around from bar to bar making matches. ***O Yeah,*** we'd say coming away with cash he'd count in his lap if he weren't too drunk.

On other days, he'd take me to other bars, & I'd sit on his knee & pretend to be someone else's little girl, &

if a man would buy him a drink, I'd let him touch my breasts & If he'd give him twenty bucks, I'd go out to the truck / take down my pants / help.

O Yeah! they'd say
going up inside me.

O Yeah! **O Yeah!** they'd say
their bodies quaking.

O Yeah! O Yeah! O Yeah

Some Nights

Some nights she'd just toss her garbage off the balcony or hang her ass out the window & piss into the wind.

Other nights, high on Percodan or Nembutal or Codeine or whatever came down the road that afternoon, she'd climb the ladder to the roof & belt out a song from South Pacific or Hair or Porgy & Bess or whatever.

Some nights she'd do nothing at all.

All winter, when nights seemed hardest to bear, she'd collect snow from her window ledge, ball it up & shell the Linderman's porch which lay open & inviting one floor down across the concrete areaway.

Some nights, an image of a stiff cock in her head, she'd go down her block to Jimmies & pick a fuck from the many who gathered in this part of town.

Summer could seem unbearable: 100 in the shade & the humidity at 95. God, how she hated to sweat.

Some nights, after her fourth shower, she'd lift her leathers from her closet, clamp a helmet on her curls, swing a leg over the seat of her Harley, crank it up & blow right on through the four stoplights that held this little town together. Some nights, that is, before Hank came back again.

Today, her head nuzzled under his arm, she walks in a crouch, ready for anything. Today, just slightly scared, always on the lookout for a quick jab or bitter quip, she unwinds.

Today, she'll clean her apartment, dump the last of the spoiled lentil soup, gray beets & rusted lettuce. Today, she'll take time to shave the wayward hairs sprouting outside the confines of her designer briefs because Hank's back & god knows he could do a lot better with those muscles & his loose tongue & stories of whores & wars & schemes & scams upon which any young girl getting hot-to-trot could learn to lean or so she thinks looking into his wide brown eyes.

So they move along the boardwalk, rubbing shoulders & groping each other & maybe the dark dreams will stop & she can concentrate again, focus on feeling good again, maybe this time won't be like all the rest & maybe, just maybe, he'll get his teeth fixed & stop bringing home his latest waitress & maybe, this time, he'll give up the idea that she likes to drop her pants in public so he can show off her splendid ass as if it belonged to him & maybe, this time, she can keep it to herself, as if it were really hers, hers alone.

Does It Matter . . .

She didn't remember the last to leave,
where she hid the keys,
money for the flowers?

Who will truss the duck, stuff the goose,
assemble the casserole,
light her fire?

Will the painters find their way?

The house is filled with grieving. Aunt Sylvia dabs her eyes between shots of Cuervo Gold. Uncle Henry rummages through her underwear. Peggy, her friend from school, doesn't quite make it to the can in time. Howard & Ron bang balls back and forth across a tattered tennis net.

The lawyer begins to read her last list of commands. We're all-ears.: Husband #l's been told to leave the door ajar.

#2 will front next year's party.

There's not enough time for the rest. Some dance, some eat.

I can't stop thinking of her camping in the snow on New Year's Eve in 1982. There were white-tailed deer wandering the meadow, red hawks overhead, blue smoke shadowing the crystalline trees.

Why is everyone so upset?
It's not as if it's never happened before.
Her timing's always been lousy.

Pass the whiskey.
Make mine sour mash.

You Said, He Said

You say, that saboteur in clean jeans & a blue flannel shirt passed out the wrong map, stole your compass, lied.

You say, he folded back the petals of strange young flowers when he should have been tending yours, explored the south pole when he should have been cruising your coral reef, licked stamps for the wrong envelope.

You say, he stashed your bucks in his Big Swiss Bank, smothered the Yorkie, sucked your best years dry.

You say, you want him hunted, hog-tied, lashed in public. You say, you want his mast & all his sails torched,

You say, retribution will be yours.

*

He says, you chose blindness, waggled mutilated hands in our face, blood-tinged flagellation.

He says, you stroked the fur of dangerous neighbors, rolled your dough for shifting grifters. He says, you sucked the cherished eyeball from his guest's prize carp, dumped cabbage soup over his head-of-state. He says, you stole his prize collection of antique underwear, must stop blubbering, clean out your attic, feed alone.

He says, you should douse your head, open your eyes, stop your run for the cliff.

He says, in fact, you never had a chance.

Vacation

On the drive from the river you slept.
I spoke once or twice.
Yesterday went by unnoticed. We
skirted last month too.
A habit born of misinterpretation,
distress, a broken nose?

When you jumped on my back, nails out,
I couldn't resist a quick right-cross.
Immediate relief / You didn't crack open.
Oh, there may have been
a bit of blood.
That's to be expected.

Picnicking in May under a spacious oak
temperate & calming
outside a castle housing what's left of De Medici's
wizards
gone to flush aristocratic flesh on the Riviera
or under cover in Rio,

Santiago, Paris or Majorca. We need
a change too. I've often
thought last year would release me.
I dreamt invisibility,
wandered over mountains guiding goats,
sheep & vagabonds,

milking in the morning, sleeping only
fitfully in flawed sheets.
There's never been much interest in
coming back. Not now.
Not without the resurrection of your
kiss. You may wish

to bite back like the cornered Rottweiler
you treasured in youth.
You may rather blow up your house,
collect insurance, deny,
once & for all, our gnarly, distorted
last vacation.

Divorce

First, there was her willingness,

before discovering how imaginative she could be, her tongue, whole mouth in fact, slurping like a wet vacuum, thick body open, upside down – her exquisite devotion to detail.

Next, her willingness to a home-based tenement, tolerating the peephole, toilet down the hall & around the corner. Need to sneak out before dawn, bags packed, condoms by the gross,

spitting venom like bad wine. Gone with sheets still damp, eating scrambled eggs & hot gruel. No-turning-back is easiest with adjustments in style, nothing to hide & a shower to piss in.

Last, her whiskey swilling boyfriend stretched-out naked in the kid's room while she dumped a 1961 vintage Hermitage down sink, padded diaper bills, opened-up like a mistress to

painters sculptors & barmen, her revolving exhibit, like her sex, grounded in time, an archival repository for plundered bones.

Is It Too Late
To Give A Part to, A Heart To,
A Whole New Start Too?

[We Marvel @ The Wonders of Modern Medicine]

What a weekend: The Smokey's living out their name all gauzy & glazed with rain. Sally & Harry in front / Barbara & Bob scrunched in the back when the corner came up too fast & all-hell-broke-loose, launching livers, bones & kidneys down the halls of U T Med Center. Sally – gone at 22 – All gone. *Except* – her heart, that fine young engine thumping out its rhythm to a step she'll never dance, scooped-up in an Igloo cooler, flown immediately to Michigan & planted, like a germinating seed, inside her aging dad. A gift he'd never wish – now ignites his future – powers his, once denied, possibilities. They say, he'd been waiting to replace that failing pump for 20 years – since Sally was 2. That was then & Now like Siamese twins, Chet & Sally eternally entwined, heart for heart: father/brother/sister – the living remnant of what was, what has & what will become. In time, when he confides: "My heart's heavy as a stone," his load may be lifted by the light she's given, that unexpected gift weightless as the air she breathes no more.

Reconciliation

If you show yourself
    promises we've made may need revision.
I remember April
    setting melon seeds in mud
photo of your face
    posed behind pink coral
Onions sets – 2 inches apart
    Never take lunch seriously

There were days of chasing fire
    Follow your compass
Trenching
    Watch the clock
Checking your list
    Time out for a cold one
Apologies
    Maybe a nap.

It often comes at an awkward pace
    from day to day
Something like that
    Or later
Joining hands /why not
    A note may suffice
Kiss & make up
    There's no turning back

Watch for a clear opening
 Death clears the decks
I've read your letters again
 April 27th always infuriates
Likewise the I Ching
 Not Roulette
Maybe not immediately
 Keno
Maybe never.

Coming To Grips

He plants green beans, broccoli &
kale over last year's squash.
65yrs 70 who can tell
his eyes crinkle in
soft October
light..

Sucking his pipe like a root he digs deep
scattering shavings, rotted fish,
chicken shit & grass,
layering earth
notching a
trough.

Worthy of worms his tactics
cajole butterflies &
bees, in the wings
weevils, dung
beetles,
slugs.

Last winter's rains decimated seedlings,
fouled streams, haystacks, pens.
Leaning against his porch
he chews his pipe hard
unwraps his
stone.

Sharpens shears & hoes, strokes the cat –
a well-known hunter, keeper of
peace. The spring will be
dry, he says, sets
drip-lines
carves

an elegant goose from a cherished walnut stash.
After 50 years, out-lasting rising rivers,
earthquakes & scorching draughts,
he makes his cuts exact
& energetically
alive.

Grandfather Benjamin

All these years I only knew you mute. Maybe your thick Russian accent, limited English,
more likely,
your son's undisguised resentment.

But you spoke brilliantly with dogs & when ours, a small Springer Spaniel whose name I've forgotten, came to heat, you locked her in the summer house, setting yourself in a chair with cane in hand to head-off stray males who were sure to come.

You stayed all afternoon & well into dusk daring the determined to 'come and get it.' Until one did, big & blotched & shaggy, at a run, twenty yards from your perch where you followed him with your eyes raising your cane & rapping a string of Russian curses each time he'd wheel.

When the sun set, you'd take her out for a walk on a short leash then lock her in when the coast was clear. Your dinner was cold but you didn't seem to care & kept the same routine until her season passed.

What did you fear for her? Certainly, not the sex or pups: *They say, you once raised sleek & silky Irish Setters on scraps*) Maybe a distrust of mongrels, reminders of your youth in the shtetls of Odessa where the Cossacks reined & Jews, always apprehensive, were only safe among their own?

Hunkering Down

The bees have already gone. Migrating ducks pass across the sun in their familiar V,

the local grocer cuts, stacks & stores a winter's worth of wood under his stairs,

wisteria sags on its trellis where it ranged at will two months before. Cats from the summer

make new homes in the barn while the neighbor's gelding begins to show a gnarled coat & apple pie replaces dewberry.

We begin to notice potatoes again. Yellow, purple, red & russet, roasted with chicken, beef & oven-braised lamb.

We begin again, casting for salmon, dismembering & dressing rabbits, the first deer.

By the time snow closes the road to all except skis & our big webbed shoes, we're *hunkering down.*

Time to corral the stock & sort what's harvested & cached. Time too for the Grizzly to den, dream of a fist full of trout. & the dazzling waters of March.

Mother Says

I want to talk about water but first mother adjusts her teeth, not wanting us to notice her collapsed mouth all chin & cheek.

She pretends to be oblivious to the pain in her shoulder but can't sit-up in bed. She says she's OK, asks for her comb & mirror.

I want to talk about water but mother says

she's lost without her watch & what have I done with her diamond ring & why is she here in this new place without her friends, her bedroom set, her privacy.

She's awakened at 5 AM to change her diaper, wash & dress. Breakfast begins at 6 & takes all morning. *Guests* arrive guided by strong, young assistants. Some are fed by hand.

Water comes to mind in her eyes
beads along her lids
dancing.

A shower is now a luxury. Once a week. It takes two attendants. She would rather be playing bingo with her cronies from across town . . .

Maybe she'll introduce "May I" or "Twist".

She sips fresh water through a blue plastic straw, rummages her relics, lifts, one after another: her silver & ivory comb & brush, her husband's 1930's vintage gavel from his Masonic lodge, the silk, lace & flowered gown she'd worn on her wedding night.

Today, she holds the photo of her mother ringed by her four daughters. She's the oldest, thick curls frame her face, fingers steady on her mother's shoulder.

As she begins to doze, her hands instinctively reach out as if to fix that old scene in time, resurrect the moment, maybe joke again with Henrietta, console the weaker Sylvia, maybe

rest her head on her mother's arm . . . as if she might, one last time, find herself at home.

She Cooked For Them In Her Own Way

She cooked for them in her own way, beating her eggs with great strokes of her whip,

scattering fists full of chopped cilantro, diced pimentos, grated gorgonzola, slivered shallots, sautéed shrimp, bacon.

Before anyone had even begun to stir, she'd have the melons skinned, berries sliced & marinating in their sweet juice,

bowls of toasted oats & almonds swimming in fresh goat's milk, muffins, jam.

By noon she'd have the plucking done: pinfeathers, feet, the dangling head.

She'd strip out globs of fat, any sign of blood. Douse with a good claret, garlic, ginger, rosemary, salt.

She'd usually choose broccoli, a simple vegetable, steamed with chive-butter & rice for starch: a mix of red, brown,

white & wild tossed with parsley, onion, cumin, saffron & garlic in boiling stock.

Her salads dazzled: spinach, jicama, radicchio, arugula, endive, romaine; escarole, carrot, celery, cabbage, scallion,

radish; walnuts, currants, tomatoes tossed with lemon, mustard, dill & olive oil.

Late in the afternoon, she'll light her fire, lay her roast on a well-greased rack, careful to save its bath for sauce,

sprinkling liberally with Herbs de Provence, black pepper & Spanish smoked paprika.

**

It's then she rests & waits / for the sun to set & footsteps to sound on the pavement under her window & she will listen for the distinct sound of yours & hers & theirs returning & one will knock & she'll open the door & greet the night with a welcoming smile & when the rich aromas have been acknowledged & coats collected, she'll invite you all to sit & when the mood is just right, she'll uncork an ancient Cote de Beaune & offer a toast to all the sharing to be & the sharing to be done.

Confronting The News

We used to wonder where war lived, what it was that made it so vile. And now we realize that we know where it lives, that it is inside ourselves.

Albert Camus: 1939

Confronting The News Today

Homage to Paul Carroll after re-reading his "Ode To Severn Darden . . ."

feels like coming into a room where someone you love is talking intimately with someone you hate

receiving a letter from & old friend who has never written before but who you've thought of often & whose death you dreamt of just last night

like knowing a young girl's being sold to men by her father

or coming to visit your son who returned from Europe three months ago but neglected to call to let you know

Confronting The News Today feels like making love to a lover from your past who has forgotten your name & all your prior couplings

hearing a voice that reminds you of the affectations of your first wife who you've come to detest

like eating the most celebrated item from a restaurant's dinner selection only to find it over-sauced, under-done & cold

or hearing your (unbearably) autocratic father will be coming to stay the summer

or having to deworm your new puppy by hand - every week for a month.

Confronting The News Today feels like smelling the last rose of summer in a doctor's office where you've come to determine whether or not the growth on your back is malignant or benign

or tasting shit on the lip of your pet dog who you'd always suspected of eating her feces but never had proof

or discovering no angel can dance on the head of a pin & that, in fact, angels can't dance, or

trying to sexually satisfy that especially new & exciting girlfriend but you can't sustain your erection.

Confronting The News feels like mistaking a skunk for an affectionate stray cat & sweeping it up in your arms

or joining a club that searches for lost children only to find the leader to be a pedophile

or like opening your refrigerator after you've been away for a month without knowing while you were gone your electric power had been disconnected.

The news feels like offering to assist a wobbly alcoholic to cross the street only to have him unceremoniously vomit on your shoes

or waking suddenly from a dream in which you were about to climax inside someone you love only to find your home engulfed in flames.

or like hearing your name had been selected from a hat to win the local lottery but you weren't home to take the call or finding your wife's been shacking-up with her karate instructor while you've been working an extra job to buy her a real mink coat.

Confronting The News Today feels like it's time to consider an extended vacation (read: permanent move) to some ancient city born of an enlightened civilization very far away, where you don't speak the language & cannot read the local paper.

Teenage Mom Drops Baby From Window

For Gloria Sosa who came to salvage what was left

Not fiction from *choice* lit
no tabloid headline
no joke

this muddled kid ditched her,
tossed naked tumbling,
straight out

Medics come, lay on hands
sew her shattered skull
patch skin

"Zoe," say the nurses
"Zoe" meaning *life*

Any day

stung blind by *No Recourse* – stoned or sober
sister-in-waiting

Every day

You Conceive It – We Own It

Any day

Many more / Will sail-out / Many more
The nation's clock is ticking

Every day

Tick Tock / Tick Tock

Today

When Arturo took one in the groin for Tammy Ray all hell broke loose.

Generally calm Paulito told his PO to fuck-off, scored a piece
from outta town
& went to work.

There are those who'd tell you
"No one knew" & "Who'd you believe" & . . .

If they'd found him early enough, he might have had a
living chance

If they'd cared enough they might have been on time
If his car hadn't made a wrong turn

If the party'd been canceled
If he or you or I . . .

There are those with dark money & debts to politicians
There are those whose mother's had made promises
There are those who can never come home

Not in this life

Not in this town

Not on this block

Not today.

Mother Ellie . . .

Was it her step-father's sticky fingers, Uncle Jim doing that thing
with his tongue or just another scum bag hustler
corn-holing her son
that did it.

Whatever doesn't really matter / Does it.

The facts are clear . . . She pulled her semiautomatics 25
drew a bead & emptied the clip, just like that
bapbapbapbapbapbap & missed just once
Just - Like - That!

While her defense fund grows, Mother Ellie walks . . .
"Nice shooting, Ellie" proclaim the T-shirts
Nice Shooting Ellie . . . Nice Ellie . . . Nice

*

In Ukraine, gunner Taras Koval reminisces in rhyme:

This is my rifle
This is my gun
This is for killing
This is for fun

But . . . Rhyming doesn't summon sex / Death-all-round

Still - He never complained

& what a lover he had been – Comic too – It's said he liked a tasty *dirty joke* & would still.
Had he survived.

*

On to Waco, Texas & **David Koresh** & the kill or be killed among us.

Good lord won't you buy me a bigger Big Gun
My friends all have pistols & want to have fun
Good lord won't you buy me bazookas & tanks
My friends all have bibles & want to give thanks.

The stand-off last 51 days
82 killed

Good-bye David, see you on the other side.

*

& what did our neighbor Jung (Sam) Woo think after making love to his wife that cool California morning, stopping for coffee & an Egg Mc-Muffin, arriving at his bicycle shop just in time to die?

The kid with the 22 Auto was quick & Sam was probably shocked outta his shorts ... Don't you think?

*

Is this the David thing, are we in the time of the David, the David-time-to-die-David time?

It was Dr. David Gunn, gunned down on his way to separate
one body from one mistake & was Taken . . . By plan
out-of-the-way.

*

& . . . In Utica or Miami, Chicago, Phoenix or Seattle,
Howard or Dave or Beth come grinning from kitchen or bedroom
saying,

"How's this look, hon?"

Wrapping lips around the blue steel barrel of a cocked 38
just before squeezing one off & permanently rearranging

once & for all time

our antiquated concept of decor.

In Memoriam - For the 100's that have died from mayhem issued from the barrel of a gun

Letter To Jason

(Reconstruction: Somewhere near Zenica, Bosnia-Herzegovina)

dozers groom the trenches, backhoes scoop & stack
the bloated bodies

After two years
dodging checkpoints,
hauling water, lumber, nails
we're teased with promises of peace
& with it
your quick return.

Then came the truth of Vukovar:
Interrogation tables slick with tongues,
Its women pawned, Kids
blown apart,
their husks hauled off by dogs.

It's said, the animals in the zoo ate their kind then died –
Simple Survival.

*

What is the instinct here?
Does the general's mother sweat,
Does the butcher's family weep,
Who sings the song of Vukovar?

*

You & your crew
grab a bite,
chart your next run,
Smoke.

*

Your eyes sag
you've developed a twitch.
Your cheekbones
glow white
in the weak light
of this shattered coffeehouse.

*

I imagine, as any father might, leaving with you
being of some fundamental use
offering protection
hefting your bag
anything

But

As your convoy gathers
one more time

tarps & tools loaded
one more time

I know
all too well
this is the trip
you've come to make
alone.

I Carry The Dead

I carry the dead child in my pack
    with dried fish my canteen
& a sealed tin of plums.

I carry his bloody shirt in my belt
    his favorite toy
a pup he'd had since birth
    over my shoulder
its eyes jiggle & snap
    its stuffing leaks
it knocks against my ribs with every step.

I raised this child
    from his mother's arms
washed his puckered skin
    combed dust from his hair
picked crusted tears from under his eyes
    pearls of shit that clung in strands to his stubby legs.

I bear this boy with a hunter's grace
    careful to measure my stride
conserving breath
    past men eating fire
past manicured lawns
    past peddlers of teeth.

I take this stiff corpse
    no more than one year old
to dig his grave beyond the trees
    where his people grazed sheep
honed tools, married & birthed

under bows of flowers
    where a stream may
at any moment
    break through polished stone.

No More

"When I went back, I found I was the enemy"
Philip Levine: Introducing his poem, They Feed They Lion

Not love but celebration / sexual & luscious
our tongues winding round / our wet bodies
yours black mine white / our smiles bright
that August afternoon / over the bridge in Windsor
before the night Detroit went down in flames.

That month, in Chicago / my Friend, Felton Nelson,
boarded up his bottle club on South Michigan Avenue

A club where his brother & I we'd spent many a Friday night
cracking set-ups for the crowd & downing shots of J D Black
while DJ's spun 78's & 45's from the fifties.

Phil Levine found he was the enemy & so had I.

No More dropping by McKee's to hear Horace or John,
Laverne's where Howlin Wolf held court, The Stage,
Robert's, The Crown / Without a local escort.

No More goofing off on 63rd
drinking outta paper bags,
eating Bar-B-Q at 4 AM
with neighborhood friends.

No More walking around Marquette Park with Connie on my arm /
No More cruising the old neighborhood.
No More.

*

As if in sepia & slow motion: 5'10" Paxton Lumpkin dribbles past the entire Dunbar High defense for a light-fingered lay-up, Big Ben Smith, 6'5" & 250 lumbers-jabs-lurches-lunges 10 yards for the score against South Shore; Antoinette George, whose skin was only slightly darker than mine & got burnt in summer, left for pre-med at Johns Hopkins & never looked back / Even before the flames ensconced her home-turf & ours / South of the river.

*

When the fires started on west Madison & west Washington & west Monroe & west . . . You could read your daily paper by the light from a million TV's engulfed in flames from end to end / The Country / from end to end & top to bottom / The Country / from where we came / to where we went / From Danville & Portsmouth & St. Pete / From Boone & Newport The Country / uprooted & cut / Dissected, Severed, Split.

*

I've never been back to Windsor & Connie never came home. I heard she married a Manitoba lawyer who stole her money & the MGA she'd treasured since college.

Her sister left Chicago too & lives in San Diego where she teaches Karate & kick-boxing to teenage prostitutes.

The Country? Ah, The Country / The Country slides in the mist shrouding the end of the century as divided as ever & as blind.

Remembering: Chicago 1968 & U S A 2023

SWEAT, *you noticed the sweat first*

McKee's little stage always had room for giants: Jones on drums, Garrison bass, Tyner Piano & The Man himself, John Coltrane. After Miles, after drugs, years before his coronation, shirt & tie, light brown suit, just a bit rumpled & sweat, from hairline & temples, softening his eyes, hardening each shudder, spasm, honk & fart wrenched from tenor or lighter sweet soprano. Across the bar, looking up through layers of smoke, we're mesmerized & when Jimmy G begins *Out-Of-This-World* we hang on every run like racers leaning through the curves urging Him to crank-it, GO John, Take Us Out John, Drive It John & he does & they do giant stride by giant stride & the sweat comes coursing down his leathered face at will & they do it again on Tunji & Miles' Moods & the club's on its feet & the guy next to me slaps me on the back & everyone's slapping high-fives & the bartenders keep popping corks & now we're out in the street & the music comes out with us & John & Elvin & McCoy & Jimmy & we're all sweating together & it seems that it'll never stop & maybe if we're really lucky . . . it never will.

Letter To Sophia

I should have known, even before the wind had shifted &
the stench of flesh on fire peeled sweat from walls, from
the whistling in my ears, the resonant whack of cracking
spines, bodies rotting in the road.

I should have hocked my gun, torched my fatigues,
joined your neighbors for the long march out. Instead.
& I tell you this with chalk in my mouth,

I drank with the rest, took my turn in the teenage girls,
forced the sons to do dog to their mothers, yes
all this I did & more.

I should have known, when my beard turned white,
when men were forced to bite the balls from their brother
when I prayed for rain to wash semen, shit & tears to the sea,

you would never take me as I was, never kiss my eyelids
with your tongue as you did, never slip your cool hands
under my shirt, press your cheek against my naked back,
never again trust me to be clean again.

After Vukovar 1992

Maps

With a kick boxer's steely eyes former skinhead, beater of black & brown, Gregory Withrow, glowers over the upturned faces of his white brothers as they hang him on their homemade cross driving spikes through his cupped palms leaving him twitching where he dangles a bright new mouth glistening under his chin.

Greg opted out, "No Way" say his buddies.

In Nebraska the New Order worries away the long midwestern winters knitting swastika ornamented sweaters. In Niceville, Florida the Church of the Creator cranks up a bloody stew of Puerto Ricans, Cubans, Jews & Haitians. But it's the Aryan Nation hunkered down in Idaho that's sworn to destroy once-and-for-all those commie Zionists whose computer bar codes have been designed specifically to kill their Christian brethren.

Seems we're bound once again to repeat once again.

This time we'll do it to the mud people
the homos
the dikes & kikes
the spics & niggers & . . .
not the micks &wops this time.

Tommy Metzger brags of farming his southern California breeding ground. His latest recruits - The Fourth Reich Skinheads last of Long Beach, "Ain't done nothin yet, just getting started," collecting AK47's, blades, lottsa blades & steel-toed Doc Martins.

For those in the know the Ku Klux Klan is dead
Long live the KKK

"Too tame," they say,
"Too tame for today!"

In Orange County, just north of San Diego, they call it "Oakie's revenge"

In Nebraska - good old
corn-on-the-cob, pork-belly-proud, home-of-the-brave – Nebraska

What do you call it?

& So . . . It's festered & grown & Now it's called MAGA
1996 / 2016

Congratulations! You Be Gettin The Big Honcho

January 4,1995 (January 20, 2016)

The big honcho got all the answers – Yesiree, You Betcha. Knows all the whys & what-fors, Nothing left to flourish in his scheme of things, be prepared to toe-yur-line, get-up-straight, reach-the-mark, squeeze-the-juice, pop-the-cork – You Betcha . . .

The big honcho got your number & he's taking names.

*

In place of the last he's the first – Got it all writ down an settin it right: Got preachers an jailers, got strikers scared shitless, got girls bout ready to sew-it-up, got a big roll & a bigger roller, can toss the bull & cut the mustard, eats the best & beats the rest, gots you screwed & blewed fore the lights go out.

*

The Big Honcho's walkin tall today – He be struttin his stuff, takin-it-back, ballin-the-jack, Yessiree, The Big Honcho weighin in heavy, got the sheriff in his jeans, got the choir singin Dixie, got young men hackin a path & women pullin his big balloon – He be here to stay, can't stop him now, You Betcha . . . No Siree

The Big Honcho got you by the balls.

[Be warned: They come in all shapes & sizes – Every 20 Years']

Bad Actors

They come through the windows

score our polished floors with their *Insignias,* rummage our bed,
warm the cushions with their piss & farts. They zoom

up, down & over the walls, unload overworked daisy chains of
wives & sisters, old ladies & young boys.

They ride into the gloom of our TV, through wire-glass, like
silverfish, they gnaw the spine of our book of *Revelations.*

The leader drops his pants & scoots across the floor like
greased-lightning, trailing shit & blood & bits of skin.

They return always chewing, spitting, rarely swallowing, they
assess maps in search of the best road home,

decorate their torsos, cheek by jowl, stuff bombs in every orifice
– Get Off – Halfcocked.

They gorge on *homecooked* from our fine china, rally often &
will again this November.

I polish the silver & keep plenty of booze They always pay in $

My Brother Coaches Me To Make Peace

He searches for a graceful conclusion, recalls Yeats, his memory
flipped on its head, remorseful.

He's begun to speak lovingly of childhood. No longer afraid of
shadows, he reclaims the family home, bites down bile, recog-
nizes futility – its broad ax.

Me? I've always been nearsighted, glasses notching my nose,
brow furrowed. No reward
in clarity, better off half-blind, squinting

past first impressions, cultivating a refined sense of smell. Nose
mostly out of joint. Equating trouble with sanitation,

scruffy hands rouses the devil, or so it seems. No satisfaction in
cutting a new tooth for the sake of sustaining a hungry kid.

Where will you bunk when the wind comes up & each doorway's
already guarded, head by haunch by handy-dandy bricks?

When will you eat, coach, if not on Sunday with "God's Chosen"
laying on a roasting, while mom counts on a pipe or a pint?

Will we eat the peace we make like shit or money or time? Like
the winner counting chips, riffling a new deck each time another
rolls over playing dead?

Will we pass our peace like giblet gravy, shuffle platitudes like
peas, wobbly at knifepoint like soured wine?

Will a quickening pulse knock against our ears, asleep @ the
outskirts, under the skirts wherever a body lies broken,

starved or riddled with holes? Do I pass now coach, run a
reverse, end-around? Will peace score the bodies cord by cord?

Will we forget the stench?

After The War

hustlers stalk the streets, hawk their mother's pearls, their
sister's virginity, over & over,
their daughter's tender tipped up
teats . . .

After the war, we'll ignore our father's failed vision, picnic at
midnight, pose in purple robes,
ride a stallion,
eat fire.

On these nights, Shelia will cake her eyelids blue, dance on her
back, wrap her legs around my waist, arch up, muscles tense,
lick my belly,
sweat.

After the war, old men will snatch their wives from trailer parks
in Galveston or Peoria, rev-up engines long left to rust
& hit the road.

Kids, with one foot in the gutter, will step to the plate, plant their
weight & hit a big one for mom & dad, or step off the curb into
chaos, or spring off the top rung, or sail out into another night,
unmasked,
tattooed,
gone.

After the war,
The thunder you'll hear in the hills will be just that, thunder in the
hills & rain.

Hunting For Her

Women have served all these centuries as looking-glasses possessing the magic and delicious power of reflecting the figure of man at twice its natural size.

Virginia Woolf: 1929

If there hadn't been women we'd still be squatting in a cave eating raw meat, because we made civilization in order to impress our girlfriends. And they tolerated it and let us go ahead and play with our toys.

Orson Welles: 1970

Beginnings

Here is the house
    White on black.
In this City of the Angels, you can trust nothing, not even the dense erratic air.
    We were lucky, my father had a job as janitor.
Ours is essentially a tragic age, so we refuse to take it tragically.
    I go corner to corner watching changing lights.
Everything requires an explanation: Name. Age. Sexual Persuasion.
    Jose. 28. Bisexual.
No doubt, some men & women truly believe in the "beautiful madness of war."
    I've given up trying to make decisions.
I am an invisible man.
    I recall this fact at inappropriate times.
Like now.
    Without ceremony.
Mother died today.
    Hardly a leaf stirred.
Sit in the bleachers & watch the women practice.
    Friday afternoons are special.
The first clean fact.
    I've taken notice but forget quickly.
I spoke of this piece of work we were doing as "curious."
    Let me let you in on a secret.
Lillian was always in a state of fermentation.
    Our family reluctantly recognizes responsibility.
He believed he was safe.
    Dogs howled beyond the light.
Nobody could sleep.

  I should be going soon.
I am in my mother's room.
  Take my hand & wish me well.
It was as if no one had heard.
  I'll say again, "Good-bye."
I am living at the Villa Borghese.
  Breakfast begins at 6 AM.

Constructed from a collection of novel's – Their first lines

Across From Bughouse Square Randolph Scott Stops For A Beer & Courts Disaster

Remembering Dennis & Loretta Schmitz . . . R I P

On walkways thick with wads of Wrigley's Spearmint, Good & Plenty & shattered Milkduds, boys twirl matched sets of nickel-plated 44's, crowd together around the block honing the pitch of their bravado.

At 1:30 this rare sunny day in March, I wait too, packing a cold Schlitz in each pocket of my P-coat, anticipating his "aw-shucks" nonchalance quick fists (he seldom used his gun) rescuing Rita or Rhonda, tossing off his "Thank you, ma'am" before trotting into the sunset, milking the fifties.

After the triple-bill, I blink back the last glint of the setting sun, imagine slapping leather & the roar of my own 44 & head to Butch McGuire's' for a beer.

Could I be a deputy, hold to one drink, tip my hat to strangers, help ladies cross the street always say "Thank you," "Yes, sir," "Yes, ma'am" live out expectations?

Polishing my badge with the back of my thumb, I decide to skip the second Bud, downing one more shot of John Jameson to steel my resolve before back-tracking through the dark to your basement flat, stealthy, unseen & only slightly drunk.

Chopping Down Hercules

Swimming upstream,
    he held his head, shoulders &
much of his chest above the water
    She'd finally wriggled free.
Sun glints from quartz in the upper reaches
    Watching buzzards circling
She heard her mother in the waves
    Speak a little more softly
And as to a conspiracy . . .
    whisper, in fact
We believe in value
    If you'll let me lift your skirt . . .
Take your cat & shove it - In fact, take this too.
    If you're dog-tired, eat the tomato –
bite it carefully, don't let it
    squirt on your shirt
In an hour, they'll bury his ass or die in the attempt.
    Trouble?
Don't give me that 'more sacred than god' argument.
    In this very room
She returned with barely enough time to pack
    The tide had reversed & the sun was folding into the hills
Is it your business?
    Would you care?
Save some for the rest of us or get out of town
    Have you been waiting long?
So long
    Here
So long
    I'll carry your bags.

In Those Days

walking with you for hours was not uncommon, we'd never speak relying instead on a gesture, a glance, a change of pace.

We'd walk for better than two hours ***In Those Days***. You filmed a biker downing a beer, that soaring eagle, even a dead porcupine.

In Those Days**,** taking your tentative hand reminded me of planting tomatoes in the rain, swimming naked under the Golden Gate Bridge.

In Those Days, I'd occasionally find you juggling limes or teasing your young collie or bargaining for blood oranges.

In Those Days you'd reminisce about your dad tossing fire-crackers to frighten passing nuns, Jim's suicide after finishing his first bronze horse.

In Those Days holding you at arms-length never satisfied. Like a picnic without a saxophone, salami or roasted peanuts.

When our Purple Martins circled south, I'd cure a ham, bottle cider, weatherize the house. Winters were longer In Those Days.

Mother & my brother Jack would hibernate, stoking the iron stove to incubate chicks, piglets & once a calf.

You were just down the road ***In Those Days***. I could watch you hauling cut wood in your cart. They said your horse had died, mule too.

In Those Days of long afternoons & longer nights I'd comb your hair, massage your naked shoulders, the tender curve of your spine.

In Those Days, I'd hunt for rabbits, anticipating the gathering of the cousins for the annual two-days feast. In Those Days

when you stopped coming, I thought you'd misunderstood, hoped you'd be back,

In Those Days. Before you moved to Paris or Stockholm or was it Istanbul?

Rain

As it's told, you still disappear in the rain, stretching a game
beyond wine & good manners, waiting to make
your move.

As if teasing weren't enough, you still elicit prying eyes with
your monkey mask & curious hands petting the patch
of silky hair

under your skirt. Who'd dare say you weren't a treat, sweeping
your entire body into a bundle, shuffling up our street,
bags ballooning, your

foreign umbrella intriguing with its stitched array of penguins.
I've collected signatures for the appeal, crystal earrings, soap.
I've done the chores

by the book: booking your private compartment, dinner in your
club-car, clean sheets & a bottle of well-aged Calvados. I've taken
samples of your saliva,

breath & skin, dusted off your collection of porcelain dolls, called
ahead for climbing gear. On days like this, when rain falls intermittently,
I walk between

the drops & remember a classy party on your dock, skipping
stones into the setting sun, sucking your tongue
in the dark.

I'm reminded how easy you'd give sex for money or your name
in the papers. Too much attention from dad?
Not enough?

I'm told the skies will clear by midnight, tomorrow will warm the
house. Should I stir the pot, light the lamp?
Will you climb

back here in time, wash your neck, polish your teeth, settle for
the rising sun & what it might bring next to a fractured &
fragmented life?

This Garden These Koi

for Josephine & Denny Zeitlin

They've been with us several years,
they eat from our hands,
lift their curved lips (ever so slightly)
They suck our fingers.

We stretch out along the edge of the pond
dangle a free hand in the cool water.

With the other, we stroke each other's neck
occasionally nibbling here & there.

This garden these Koi, hyacinth, lavender,
mist in late afternoon,
the salient rhythms of falling water.

This garden these Koi
my hand along your back
your fingers in my mouth.

Wood-Shedding

For Denny Zeitlin

While Escondido wilts in unseasonable heat, tight-assed & bitter
adolescent kids, sneak under our fence to smoke & fuck

inside the broken-down shed just west of my own disguised retreat.

I'd like to think, my time, so seductively spent. I'd like to think,
this hiding-out, this *Wood-Shedding*, stokes high drama &
butters the crisp sourdough of language.

Like a proud Kentucky miner, I sport a snakeskin jacket, rum-
mage this high-desert like a bear, sharpening notes, honing
harmonies, extracting the essence.

It is, after all, a solo performance.

So, while the kids next-door screech in the heat of their salacious
discoveries, I stroke the gentle curve of some mythical back &
pick at words

too mute to celebrate themselves, too timid to initiate their own
seduction.

Woodshedding: Musicians privately honing their craft [Writers too]

The Beginning Of The End

I spent the day before the wedding with Roberta. She'd dropped in to say good-bye, her ever present carpetbag brimming with antiquated treasures.

As I packed, she offered them up: A satin purse, its bright blue lining torn, its belly plump with plums.

A small black box held her great-uncle's onyx ring, a blood red scarf, a diamond stud she'd set in a lion's tooth.

She sifted through her bag for one last gift, pausing now & then to loosen layers of her clothes.

It was a startlingly inventive afternoon.

beginning when I kissed the thick-tipped breasts that were her mother's gift, kissed the plump lips she shared with her sister.

From beneath the glistening swatch of her pubic hair, the slick, sculpted caress of her vagina reached up – drawing me in.

She especially enjoyed my tongue opening for it to reach more & further as she slid herself along its edge keeping it wet with her own wet.

Her low slung buttocks flexed & relaxed keeping a beat at their center. Her asshole winking with each twitch of her hip.

We gorged ourselves: Picnicking like gluttons, sucking the juices, licking our platters clean.

It was at that moment, with no time to change tickets or sell my ride, I left for the train convinced – I was entering the *beginning-of-the-end*

& so it was

Sue

Your stark, bald head still embarrasses, your wrinkled gown still flaps at will against your shell.

Your last question, "Why must we be sick?" still echoes through your morphine haze as poignant & naive as it did at S F General the day you died.

We'd grown close, your sculpted forms enticing poems, long spontaneous afternoons our private time replete.

The ceramic gull you tentatively balanced on one crippled leg, still guards its perch above my desk, your welcoming vagina, fired as a joke, broke when I moved away.

Last week, I imagined seeing you, one last time, blond hair swept high in silhouette, scanning the waves for Gray Whales heading south. When, seemingly on cue,

one magnificently mottled body hurtled through the air in a playful breach, blinked a teasing eye, arched its fluke & dove though parting waves, determined to go on

I'm living near Mexico now. You'd love its sensuality: dark, young men, long hours in the sun, time

to dive the virgin reefs off Baja, time to sculpt, time to haunt the beaches incommunicado, free & innocent again.

In Memory of Sue Volstead R I P

A Short Time After

A Short Time After Wendy & Bob disappeared in Zaire & Mike died in a train wreck outside Albuquerque, you came from the mist,

worn down by too much touch & go, from running to escape a torrent of nightmares of the Boom & Bap of gunfire, of arms & legs & torsos torn & dead kids dead.

After your mom moved to the basement & your dad ran off with Arlene, you came home one blustery November afternoon
& blew yourself away.

Your kid brother, Jake, hauling fish in Oregon or Barry, good-old-loving Barry, sweating out the last thirty minutes on his jack-hammer, could never claim your act for a lesson learned or risk taken.

It's different for me, collecting seeds from the last sunflowers, cuttings from roses, the ripest melon. It's always been different for me. I know rain's not far off & some afternoons are not worth re-living.

But now, even with a good dog & the latest compass, I've not been able to find my way in the dark. Let alone – after all these years – leave the memory of you . . . Alive & Dead.

You'd Come Back. Wouldn't You

Come on. Sit beside me. It's O K. We'll remember other times. Nine years. Right? But. Who's counting? It was & we were &

what I crave now is to revive the memory – Rest my head on your shoulder & feel the crinkled silk of your blouse against my cheek.

I can't quite tell. Did we really relish the fucking or just sniffing around. I know I took to your haunch like a burly pup licking here & licking there.

Madrid, wasn't it? That fall, when all the guests were gone & cats came back to rustle scraps behind Eduardo's Bar. Yes! There we are.

You've got your hand up my shirt rubbing my bare back, keeping me close, while I caress your voluptuous & tantalizing ass.

Did we ever come to grips or was that the time your sister came between us flying in from Bermuda with her barber in tow & that fancy way with her tongue.

Maybe – look instead at London & the Ivanhoe with its temperamental laundress & the maid who did us both. You tried hashish

for the first time, while I crawled the walls on crystal meth. Did that dancer from Dublin really *loan* you the 5 pounds? Wait! I know. It's too late for that.

Here. Take my hand. We'll walk to the end of the pier. Seals
asleep on the crossbeams. Their baying calms the suicidal.
Watch your step. The slats can be slick. I hate

knowing I could lose you again. But, I saw him lunching in your
lobby & heard his ship's booked to leave tomorrow on the turning
tide.

By No Means

I laid out two suits, underwear, socks, shirts & ties. Packed my trunk.
    Never thinking how long it would take.

I'm not an impartial observer.
    Notice the lit cigar in my hand.

I knew you didn't know me.
    Were the bodies simply buried?

I'd passed visibly through two states &
    was entering a third.

A hot wind came from nowhere.
    I drove him

he wanted to go.
    Truth is not lost on the deaf.

Black men worked the field.
    Pick only ripe fruit.

Searching the kitchen. I didn't see.
    Under the stairs

the wooden tub &
    him in it.

You sleep. I'll drive.
    As if he wasn't there.

This may be the time
    to step back.

She's alone on the first stool,
    how nice it would be

to get you drunk
    & take you home,

we would fuck on the sofa in the den.
    I could do this.

Deep down
    it was all the same to me.

Hunting For Her

I was hunting for her when her husband answered the door. His niece, I think it was, hovered at his shoulder while he grilled *the interloper.*

.

It seems, she'd flown off with some credentialed scribbler from Australia, nice chap we'd meet later at the capital . . . *But. That's another story.*

Back to the interrogation with the sparks flying & the hot-sauce being liberally applied & the niece, hawk billed she was &

pinched to popping in her proper print with its high neck, still hovering & he, almost casually at the pit, turning-up the heat, then down, then up again . . . Offering drinks.

The last time I'd seen her she was basking naked in a gondola with John Coltrane playing his tenor in her ear.

It seems, after all their time, he'd never been on those rides. Afraid of water, I guess, or jazz in general. Whatever possessed them to marry?

Something about her father, him being so much older? It's clear, they were never sure of their routing or even how to map it.

Never a girl scout, she did have a knack for exploration & erecting provocative structures. I'll never forget the thickest, silkiest, most astonishingly luxurious pubic hair, her slightly raspy, when-well-oiled voice coaxing . . .

These days she lives in Israel between war & peace & rationing. Believe it or not, there are now the three of them (don't ask me how or why).

& Me? I'm having it down south & far away with a woman who really knows how to scout the territory, keep the fire low, hot & well-tended.

Other Books By Roger Aplon

Stiletto
By Dawn's Early Light at 120 Miles Per Hour
It's Mother's Day [Original version]
Barcelona Diary
The Man With His Back To The Room
Intimacies – Prose poems & Stories
After Goya – *chapbook* *
Improvisations – *chapbook*
Escapades – *chapbook* ***
It's Only TV
Improvisations – From Contemporary Music
Homage To A Widow – *chapbook* ***
Mustering What's Left
The omnipotent Sorcerer
After Goya & Selected New Poems * (*chapbook included*)
Burn Baby Burn *** (2 *chapbooks included*)
Beethoven Project

www.ingramcontent.com/pod-product-compliance
Lightning Source LLC
Chambersburg PA
CBHW050022170726
48282CB00025B/509
* 9 7 8 8 1 1 9 2 2 8 0 2 7 *